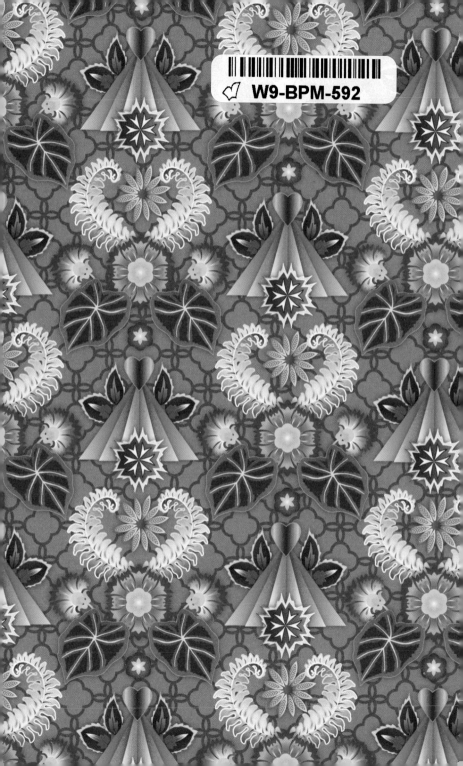

W9-BPM-592

COURAGE

PERSONAL INFORMATION

NAME

ADDRESS

HOME TELEPHONE   MOBILE

E-MAIL

BUSINESS ADDRESS

TELEPHONE

FAX

E-MAIL

WEBSITE

DOCTOR   TELEPHONE

BLOOD TYPE   RH   ALLERGIES

VACCINES   VALID UNTIL

VACCINES   VALID UNTIL

VACCINES   VALID UNTIL

IDENTITY CARD NO.   VALID UNTIL

PASSPORT   VALID UNTIL

ISSUED ON

VISA   VALID UNTIL

VISA   VALID UNTIL

DRIVER'S LICENSE   VALID UNTIL

CAR REGISTRATION NO.

MOTORCYCLE REGISTRATION NO.

BANK ACCOUNT NO.

CREDIT CARD   VALID UNTIL

MEDICAL INSURANCE COMPANY

TRAVEL INSURANCE

IN CASE OF ACCIDENT PLEASE NOTIFY

NAME

ADDRESS   TELEPHONE

PAULO COELHO

COURAGE

Day Planner
2016

Vintage International
Vintage Books
A Division of Penguin Random House LLC
New York

COURAGE

They are virtues we hear about every day
and that we can practice in every moment.
Patience: Love is patient...
Kindness: ...and kind.
Generosity: Love does not envy...
Humility: ...or boast; it is not arrogant...
Courtesy: ...or rude.
Unselfishness: It does not insist on its own way.
Good temper: It is not irritable...or resentful.
Guilelessness: *or resentful.*
Sincerity: It does not rejoice at wrongdoing,
but rejoices with the truth.

ADULTERY

2016

JANUARY

S	M	T	W	T	F	S
					1	2
3	4	5	6	7	8	9
10	11	12	13	14	15	16
17	18	19	20	21	22	23
24	25	26	27	28	29	30
31						

1 New Year's Day
18 Martin Luther King Day

FEBRUARY

S	M	T	W	T	F	S
	1	2	3	4	5	6
7	8	9	10	11	12	13
14	15	16	17	18	19	20
21	22	23	24	25	26	27
28	29					

14 Valentine's Day
15 Presidents Day

MARCH

S	M	T	W	T	F	S
		1	2	3	4	5
6	7	8	9	10	11	12
13	14	15	16	17	18	19
20	21	22	23	24	25	26
27	28	29	30	31		

25 Good Friday
27 Easter

APRIL

S	M	T	W	T	F	S
					1	2
3	4	5	6	7	8	9
10	11	12	13	14	15	16
17	18	19	20	21	22	23
24	25	26	27	28	29	30

MAY

S	M	T	W	T	F	S
1	2	3	4	5	6	7
8	9	10	11	12	13	14
15	16	17	18	19	20	21
22	23	24	25	26	27	28
29	30	31				

8 Mother's Day
30 Memorial Day

JUNE

S	M	T	W	T	F	S
			1	2	3	4
5	6	7	8	9	10	11
12	13	14	15	16	17	18
19	20	21	22	23	24	25
26	27	28	29	30		

19 Father's Day

JULY

S	M	T	W	T	F	S
					1	2
3	4	5	6	7	8	9
10	11	12	13	14	15	16
17	18	19	20	21	22	23
24	25	26	27	28	29	30
31						

4 Independence Day

AUGUST

S	M	T	W	T	F	S
	1	2	3	4	5	6
7	8	9	10	11	12	13
14	15	16	17	18	19	20
21	22	23	24	25	26	27
28	29	30	31			

SEPTEMBER

S	M	T	W	T	F	S
				1	2	3
4	5	6	7	8	9	10
11	12	13	14	15	16	17
18	19	20	21	22	23	24
25	26	27	28	29	30	

5 Labor Day

OCTOBER

S	M	T	W	T	F	S
						1
2	3	4	5	6	7	8
9	10	11	12	13	14	15
16	17	18	19	20	21	22
23	24	25	26	27	28	29
30	31					

10 Columbus Day
31 Halloween

NOVEMBER

S	M	T	W	T	F	S
		1	2	3	4	5
6	7	8	9	10	11	12
13	14	15	16	17	18	19
20	21	22	23	24	25	26
27	28	29	30			

11 Veteran's Day
24 Thanksgiving

DECEMBER

S	M	T	W	T	F	S
				1	2	3
4	5	6	7	8	9	10
11	12	13	14	15	16	17
18	19	20	21	22	23	24
25	26	27	28	29	30	31

25 Christmas Day

2017

JANUARY

S	M	T	W	T	F	S
1	**2**	3	4	5	6	7
8	9	10	11	12	13	14
15	**16**	17	18	19	20	21
22	23	24	25	26	27	28
29	30	31				

1 New Year's Day
16 Martin Luther King Day

FEBRUARY

S	M	T	W	T	F	S
			1	2	3	4
5	6	7	8	9	10	11
12	13	14	15	16	17	18
19	**20**	21	22	23	24	25
26	27	28				

14 Valentine's Day
20 Presidents Day

MARCH

S	M	T	W	T	F	S
			1	2	3	4
5	6	7	8	9	10	11
12	13	14	15	16	17	18
19	20	21	22	23	24	25
26	27	28	29	30	31	

APRIL

S	M	T	W	T	F	S
						1
2	3	4	5	6	7	8
9	10	11	12	13	**14**	15
16	17	18	19	20	21	22
23	24	25	26	27	28	29
30						

14 Good Friday
16 Easter

MAY

S	M	T	W	T	F	S
	1	2	3	4	5	6
7	8	9	10	11	12	13
14	15	16	17	18	19	20
21	22	23	24	25	26	27
28	**29**	30	31			

14 Mother's Day
29 Memorial Day

JUNE

S	M	T	W	T	F	S
				1	2	3
4	5	6	7	8	9	10
11	12	13	14	15	16	17
18	19	20	21	22	23	24
25	26	27	28	29	30	

18 Father's Day

JULY

S	M	T	W	T	F	S
						1
2	3	**4**	5	6	7	8
9	10	11	12	13	14	15
16	17	18	19	20	21	22
23	24	25	26	27	28	29
30	31					

4 Independence Day

AUGUST

S	M	T	W	T	F	S
		1	2	3	4	5
6	7	8	9	10	11	12
13	14	15	16	17	18	19
20	21	22	23	24	25	26
27	28	29	30	31		

SEPTEMBER

S	M	T	W	T	F	S
					1	2
3	**4**	5	6	7	8	9
10	11	12	13	14	15	16
17	18	19	20	21	22	23
24	25	26	27	28	29	30

4 Labor Day

OCTOBER

S	M	T	W	T	F	S
1	2	3	4	5	6	7
8	**9**	10	11	12	13	14
15	16	17	18	19	20	21
22	23	24	25	26	27	28
29	30	31				

9 Columbus Day
31 Halloween

NOVEMBER

S	M	T	W	T	F	S
			1	2	3	4
5	6	7	8	9	**10**	**11**
12	13	14	15	16	17	18
19	20	21	22	**23**	24	25
26	27	28	29	30		

11 Veteran's Day
23 Thanksgiving

DECEMBER

S	M	T	W	T	F	S
					1	2
3	4	5	6	7	8	9
10	11	12	13	14	15	16
17	18	19	20	21	22	23
24	**25**	26	27	28	29	30
31						

25 Christmas Day

2016 YEAR PLANNER

JANUARY

F	1
S	2
S	**3**
M	4
T	5
W	6
T	7
F	8
S	9 ●
S	**10**
M	11
T	12
W	13
T	14
F	15
S	16 ◑
S	**17**
M	18
T	19
W	20
T	21
F	22
S	23 ○
S	**24**
M	25
T	26
W	27
T	28
F	29
S	30
S	**31** ◐

FEBRUARY

M	1
T	2
W	3
T	4
F	5
S	6
S	**7**
M	8 ●
T	9
W	10
T	11
F	12
S	13
S	**14**
M	15 ◐
T	16
W	17
T	18
F	19
S	20
S	**21**
M	22 ○
T	23
W	24
T	25
F	26
S	27
S	**28**
M	29

MARCH

T	1 ◐
W	2
T	3
F	4
S	5
S	**6**
M	7
T	8 ●
W	9
T	10
F	11
S	12
S	**13**
M	14
T	15 ◐
W	16
T	17
F	18
S	19
S	**20**
M	21
T	22
W	23 ○
T	24
F	25
S	26
S	**27**
M	28
T	29
W	30
T	31 ◐

APRIL		
F	1	
S	2	
S	**3**	
M	4	
T	5	
W	6	
T	7	●
F	8	
S	9	
S	**10**	
M	11	
T	12	
W	13	
T	14	◐
F	15	
S	16	
S	**17**	
M	18	
T	19	
W	20	
T	21	
F	22	○
S	23	
S	**24**	
M	25	
T	26	
W	27	
T	28	
F	29	◑
S	30	

MAY		
S	**1**	
M	2	
T	3	
W	4	
T	5	
F	6	●
S	7	
S	**8**	
M	9	
T	10	
W	11	
T	12	
F	13	◐
S	14	
S	**15**	
M	16	
T	17	
W	18	
T	19	
F	20	
S	21	○
S	**22**	
M	23	
T	24	
W	25	
T	26	
F	27	
S	28	
S	**29**	◑
M	30	
T	31	

JUNE		
W	1	
T	2	
F	3	
S	4	●
S	**5**	
M	6	
T	7	
W	8	
T	9	
F	10	
S	11	
S	**12**	◐
M	13	
T	14	
W	15	
T	16	
F	17	
S	18	
S	**19**	
M	20	○
T	21	
W	22	
T	23	
F	24	
S	25	
S	**26**	
M	27	◑
T	28	
W	29	
T	30	

2016 YEAR PLANNER

JULY			AUGUST			SEPTEMBER		
F	1		M	1		T	1	●
S	2		T	2	●	F	2	
S	**3**		W	3		S	3	
M	4	●	T	4		S	**4**	
T	5		F	5		M	5	
W	6		S	6		T	6	
T	7		S	**7**		W	7	
F	8		M	8		T	8	
S	9		T	9		F	9	◐
S	**10**		W	10	◐	S	10	
M	11	◐	T	11		S	**11**	
T	12		F	12		M	12	
W	13		S	13		T	13	
T	14		S	**14**		W	14	
F	15		M	15		T	15	
S	16		T	16		F	16	○
S	**17**		W	17		S	17	
M	18		T	18	○	S	**18**	
T	19	○	F	19		M	19	
W	20		S	20		T	20	
T	21		S	**21**		W	21	
F	22		M	22		T	22	
S	23		T	23		F	23	◑
S	**24**		W	24	◑	S	24	
M	25		T	25		S	**25**	
T	26	◑	F	26		M	26	
W	27		S	27		T	27	
T	28		S	**28**		W	28	
F	29		M	29		T	29	
S	30		T	30		F	30	●
S	**31**		W	31				

OCTOBER			NOVEMBER			DECEMBER		
S	1		T	1		T	1	
S	**2**		W	2		F	2	
M	3		T	3		S	3	
T	4		F	4		S	**4**	
W	5		S	5		M	5	
T	6		S	**6**		T	6	
F	7		M	7	◑	W	7	◑
S	8		T	8		T	8	
S	**9**	◑	W	9		F	9	
M	10		T	10		S	10	
T	11		F	11		S	**11**	
W	12		S	12		M	12	
T	13		S	**13**		T	13	○
F	14		M	14	○	W	14	
S	15		T	15		T	15	
S	**16**	○	W	16		F	16	
M	17		T	17		S	17	
T	18		F	18		S	**18**	
W	19		S	19		M	19	
T	20		S	**20**		T	20	◐
F	21		M	21	◐	W	21	
S	22	◐	T	22		T	22	
S	**23**		W	23		F	23	
M	24		T	24		S	24	
T	25		F	25		S	**25**	
W	26		S	26		M	26	
T	27		S	**27**		T	27	
F	28		M	28		W	28	
S	29		T	29	●	T	29	●
S	**30**	●	W	30		F	30	
M	31					S	31	

JANUARY

Confidence

Let yourself get carried away by the night from time to time. Look up at the stars and try to get drunk on the sense of infinity. The night, with all its charms, is also a path to enlightenment. Just as a dark well has thirst-quenching water at its bottom, the night, whose mystery brings us closer to the mystery of God, has a flame capable of enkindling our soul hidden in its shadows.

ADULTERY

1 | Friday

2 | Saturday

3 | Sunday

A happy man is a man who carries God within him.
And happiness can be found in a simple grain of desert sand.

THE ALCHEMIST

4 | Monday

5 | Tuesday

The worst thing is to choose a path and then spend
the rest of your life wondering if you've made the right choice.
No one can make a choice without feeling afraid.

BRIDA

6 Wednesday

7 Thursday

8 Friday

9 Saturday

10 Sunday

We will not fear the darkness because we are partners of the light.

ADULTERY

11 Monday

12 Tuesday

Love is also a mysterious thing:
the more we give, the more it grows.

CHRONICLE: RESPECTING WORK

13 Wednesday

14 Thursday

15 Friday

16 Saturday

17 | Sunday

God is always close to us, whether we pray to him or not.

ALEPH

18 Monday

19 Tuesday

Seize the opportunity offered to you by tragedy;
not everyone can do that.

THE FIFTH MOUNTAIN

20 Wednesday

21 Thursday

22 | Friday

23 | Saturday

24 | Sunday

God is here, now, by our side. We can see him in this mist, in this
earth, in these clothes, in these shoes. His angels watch over us
while we are sleeping and help us while we are working.
In order to find God, all you need is to look around you.

BY THE RIVER PIEDRA I SAT DOWN AND WEPT

25 Monday

26 Tuesday

In order to hear Love's words, we must allow Love to approach.

MANUSCRIPT FOUND IN ACCRA

27 Wednesday

28 Thursday

29 Friday

30 Saturday

31 Sunday

Nothing in this world is useless in the eyes of God.

MANUSCRIPT FOUND IN ACCRA

FEBRUARY

Risk

Follow your dreams, and transform your life into a path
that leads to God. Perform miracles. Heal. Prophesize.
Listen to your guardian angel. Transform yourself.
Be a warrior and be happy in your fight.
Take whatever risks you need to take.

BY THE RIVER PIEDRA I SAT DOWN AND WEPT

1 Monday

2 Tuesday

3 Wednesday

4 Thursday

Forgetting is the wrong approach.
You should face things head-on.

ADULTERY

5 Friday

6 Saturday

You can't say to the Spring:
"Come now and last as long as possible."
You can only say:
"Come and bless me with your hope, and stay as long as you can."

ELEVEN MINUTES

7 Sunday

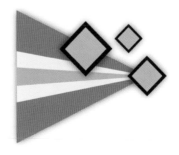

8 Monday

9 Tuesday

10 Wednesday

11 Thursday

It's good to learn that everything in life has a price.
That is what the Warriors of Light try to teach us.

THE ALCHEMIST

12 Friday

13 Saturday

Woe to those who were never beaten!
They will never be winners in this life.

MANUSCRIPT FOUND IN ACCRA

14 Sunday

15 Monday

16 Tuesday

17 Wednesday

18 Thursday

There is no tragedy, only the inevitable.
Everything has its reason for being; all you have to learn is how to
distinguish what will pass and what will last.

THE FIFTH MOUNTAIN

19 Friday

20 Saturday

Even if I learn nothing new on this path,
at least I will have learned one important thing:
we have to take risks.

BRIDA

21 Sunday

22 | Monday

23 | Tuesday

24 Wednesday

25 Thursday

What is sin? It is a sin to prevent Love from showing itself.

THE WITCH OF PORTOBELLO

26 | Friday

---

27 | Saturday

Wouldn't it be better to see challenges as a source of knowledge, and not as our enemies?

ADULTERY

28 Sunday

29 Monday

MARCH

Surrender

Contradictions are what make love grow.
Conflicts are what allow love to remain by our side.
Life is too short for us to keep important words like
"I love you" locked in our hearts.

MANUSCRIPT FOUND IN ACCRA

1 | Tuesday

2 Wednesday

3 Thursday

We love because we love.
There is no reason to love.

THE ALCHEMIST

4 Friday

5 Saturday

The problem is that people tend to relate these traits to the Love of God, but how does God's Love manifest itself?
Through the Love of man. To find Peace in the heavens,
we must find love on Earth. Without it, we are worthless.

ADULTERY

6 Sunday

7 | Monday

8 | Tuesday

9 Wednesday

10 Thursday

True love is an act of total surrender.

BY THE RIVER PIEDRA I SAT DOWN AND WEPT

11 Friday

12 Saturday

Let us love one another, but not try to possess one another.

ELEVEN MINUTES

13 | Sunday

14 | Monday

15 | Tuesday

16 Wednesday

17 Thursday

God reveals himself in any task,
but mainly in those tasks that are performed with love.

THE FIFTH MOUNTAIN

18 Friday

19 Saturday

Anyone who has the courage to say what he feels in his heart
is in touch with God.

CHRONICLE: THE TREE AND ITS FRUITS

20 | Sunday

21 Monday

22 Tuesday

23 | Wednesday

24 | Thursday

The warrior never loses sight of those things that last or of the
strong bonds that are forged over time.
He can distinguish between what will pass and what will last.

MANUAL OF THE WARRIOR OF LIGHT

25 Friday

26 Saturday

The universe only makes sense
when we have someone to share our feelings with.

ELEVEN MINUTES

27 | Sunday

28 Monday

29 Tuesday

30 Wednesday

31 Thursday

Every moment in life is an act of faith.

BRIDA

APRIL

Changes

To build or to plant. The builders might take years over their
tasks, but one day, they finish what they're doing.
Then they find they're hemmed in by their own walls.
Life loses its meaning when the building stops.
Then there are those who plant. They endure storms and all
the many vicissitudes of the seasons, and they rarely rest.
But, unlike a building, a garden never stops growing.
And while it requires the gardener's constant attention,
it also allows life for the gardener
to be a great adventure.

BRIDA

1 Friday

2 Saturday

3 | Sunday

I hope that the small things lead to great transformations.

ADULTERY

4 | Monday

5 | Tuesday

Victors never make the same mistake twice.
That is why the warrior only risks his heart for something
worthwhile.

MANUAL OF THE WARRIOR OF LIGHT

6 Wednesday

7 Thursday

8 Friday

9 Saturday

10 | Sunday

Faith and transformation are the only ways of drawing near to God.

MANUSCRIPT FOUND IN ACCRA

11 | Monday

12 | Tuesday

Life can change from one second to the next.
The right moment is always there waiting;
one's will power is constantly being put to the test.

THE WINNER STANDS ALONE

13 | Wednesday

14 | Thursday

15 Friday

16 Saturday

17 Sunday

It's never too late to live your dream.

CHRONICLE: STARTING AT 70

18 Monday

19 Tuesday

And to those who believe that adventures are dangerous,
I say, try routine; that kills you far more quickly.

MANUSCRIPT FOUND IN ACCRA

20 Wednesday

21 Thursday

22 Friday

23 Saturday

24 | Sunday

So what we call "life" is a train with many carriages.
Sometimes we're in one, sometimes we're in another,
and sometimes we cross Aleph between them, when we dream or
allow ourselves to be swept away by the extraordinary.

ALEPH

2 5 Monday

2 6 Tuesday

Wisdom and experience don't change the man.
Time doesn't change the man.
The only thing that changes us is love.

A D U L T E R Y

27 Wednesday

28 Thursday

29 Friday

30 Saturday

Love can take us to heaven or to hell,
but it will always take us somewhere.
We must accept it, because it is what nourishes our existence.

BY THE RIVER PIEDRA I SAT DOWN AND WEPT

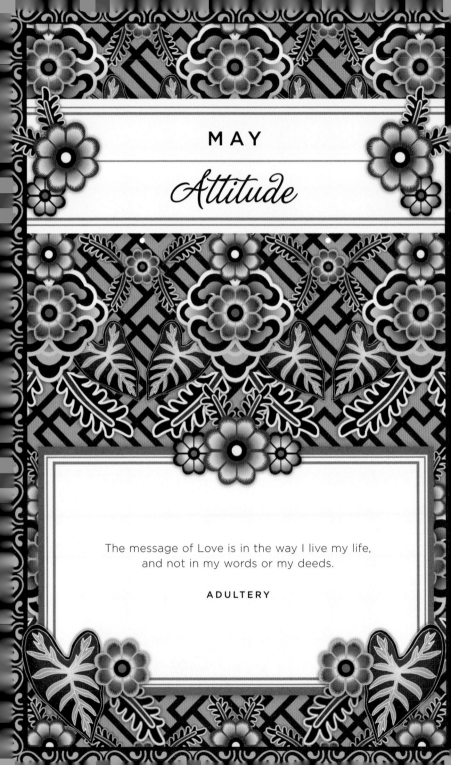

MAY

Attitude

The message of Love is in the way I live my life,
and not in my words or my deeds.

ADULTERY

1 Sunday

Not everyone who owns a pile of gold the size of that hill to the south of our city is rich. The truly rich person is the one who is in contact with the energy of Love every second of his existence.

MANUSCRIPT FOUND IN ACCRA

2 Monday

3 Tuesday

There is only one way of learning: through action.

THE ALCHEMIST

4 Wednesday

5 Thursday

6 Friday

7 Saturday

8 Sunday

The meaning of my life is the meaning I choose to give it.

THE FIFTH MOUNTAIN

9 Monday

10 Tuesday

A gift is a grace, or a mercy,
but it is also a grace knowing how to lead a dignified,
hard-working life full of love for one's fellow man.

BY THE RIVER PIEDRA I SAT DOWN AND WEPT

11 | Wednesday

---

12 | Thursday

13 Friday

14 Saturday

15 Sunday

If someone knows what he wants from life,
then he has all he needs in order to fulfill his dreams.

CHRONICLE: THE BLIND MAN AND EVEREST

16 Monday

17 Tuesday

Wisdom means both to know and to transform.

B R I D A

18 | Wednesday

19 | Thursday

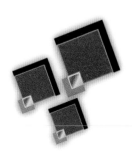

20 Friday

21 Saturday

22 | Sunday

Whenever you want to achieve something, keep your eyes open,
concentrate and know exactly what it is that you want.

THE DEVIL AND MISS PRYM

23 | Monday

24 | Tuesday

I love you because the whole Universe conspired to help me
find you.

THE ALCHEMIST

2 5 Wednesday

2 6 Thursday

27 Friday

28 Saturday

29 | Sunday

Living is making decisions and dealing with the consequences.

ADULTERY

30 Monday

31 Tuesday

Love—because you will be the first to benefit.

MANUSCRIPT FOUND IN ACCRA

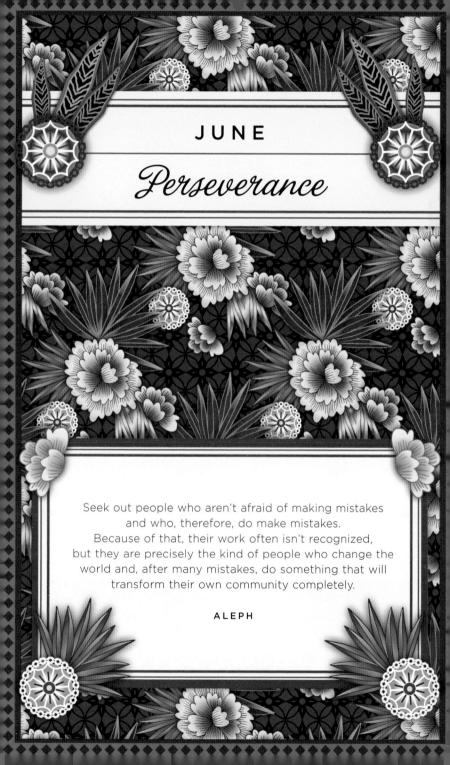

JUNE

Perseverance

Seek out people who aren't afraid of making mistakes
and who, therefore, do make mistakes.
Because of that, their work often isn't recognized,
but they are precisely the kind of people who change the
world and, after many mistakes, do something that will
transform their own community completely.

ALEPH

1 Wednesday

2 Thursday

You don't choose your life; it chooses you.
There's no point asking why life has reserved certain joys or griefs,
you just accept them and carry on.

ADULTERY

3 Friday

4 Saturday

I see that there are still many dark areas inside me,
but with perseverance and courage
they will gradually be washed away.

THE ZAHIR

5 Sunday

6 | Monday

7 | Tuesday

8 Wednesday

9 Thursday

There will never be anything physical between us,
but no passion is in vain, no love is ever wasted.
The energy of love can never be lost—it is more powerful than
anything and shows itself in many ways.

THE WITCH OF PORTOBELLO

10 | Friday

11 | Saturday

Scars speak more loudly than the sword that caused them.

MANUSCRIPT FOUND IN ACCRA

12 Sunday

13 Monday

14 Tuesday

15 Wednesday

16 Thursday

I have become aware that repeated experiences have but one purpose: to teach us that we have not yet learned the lesson.

CHRONICLE: DIALOGUES WITH MY TEACHER

17 | Friday

18 | Saturday

Love is a force that exists on earth to make us happy,
to bring us closer to God and to our fellow man.

THE ZAHIR

19 Sunday

20 | Monday

21 | Tuesday

22 | Wednesday

23 | Thursday

It is through prayers that we commune with God.
A prayer, when couched in the words of the soul,
is far more powerful than any ritual.

BRIDA

24 Friday

25 Saturday

You give but little when you give of your possessions.
It is when you give of yourself that you truly give.

THE WITCH OF PORTOBELLO

26 | Sunday

27 | Monday

28 | Tuesday

29 Wednesday

30 Thursday

The warrior knows that there are occasional pauses in the struggle. There is always something not quite right. And the warrior takes advantage of those moments when time stops to equip himself better.

MANUAL OF THE WARRIOR OF LIGHT

JULY

Enthusiasm

When the warrior of light enters the fight, all he has is his enthusiasm and the moves and strikes that he learned during his training. As the fight progresses, he discovers that enthusiasm and training are not enough to win: what counts is experience. Then he opens his heart to the Universe and asks God to give him the inspiration he needs to turn every blow from his enemy into a lesson in self-defense.

MANUAL OF THE WARRIOR OF LIGHT

1 Friday

2 Saturday

3 Sunday

Everything we seek so enthusiastically before we reach
adulthood—love, work, faith—turns into a burden too heavy to bear.
There is only one way to escape this: love.
To love is to transform slavery into freedom.

ADULTERY

4 Monday

5 Tuesday

Only Love gives form to what, once, we could not even dream of.

MANUSCRIPT FOUND IN ACCRA

6 Wednesday

7 Thursday

8 | Friday

9 | Saturday

10 | Sunday

Love is a feeling completely bound up with color,
like thousands of rainbows superimposed one on top of the other.

BRIDA

11 Monday

12 Tuesday

A child can teach an adult three things: to be happy for no reason,
to always be busy with something and to know how to demand
what he or she wants, as forcefully as possible.

THE FIFTH MOUNTAIN

13 Wednesday

14 Thursday

15 Friday

16 Saturday

17 | Sunday

The Language that the world speaks and that everyone on Earth
can understand in their hearts is the Language of Love.

THE ALCHEMIST

18 Monday

19 Tuesday

When we love and believe in something from the bottom of our
heart, in feelings that are stronger than the world itself,
we are filled by a serenity that comes from the certainty
that nothing can crush our faith.

THE PILGRIMAGE

20 | Wednesday

21 | Thursday

22 Friday

23 Saturday

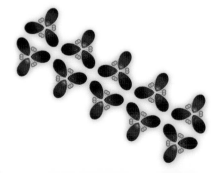

24 | Sunday

I think that when we bravely seek out love,
love reveals itself and we end up attracting even more love.

BY THE RIVER PIEDRA I SAT DOWN AND WEPT

25 Monday

26 Tuesday

Defeat is for those who, despite their fears,
live with enthusiasm and faith.
Defeat is for the valiant.
Only they will know the honor of losing and the joy of winning.

MANUSCRIPT FOUND IN ACCRA

27 | Wednesday

28 | Thursday

29 Friday

30 Saturday

31 Sunday

Anyone who is in love is making love the whole time,
even when they're not. When two bodies meet,
it is just the cup overflowing.

ELEVEN MINUTES

AUGUST

Freedom

The true experience of freedom is having the most important thing in the world without actually owning it.

ELEVEN MINUTES

1 | Monday

2 | Tuesday

3 Wednesday

4 Thursday

The moment of release is accompanied by pain,
but it's always been that way.

ADULTERY

5 | Friday
_____

6 | Saturday
_____

The simple fact of having the courage to say meaningless things
began to fill me with euphoria. I was free,
I didn't need to explain my actions. That freedom was carrying me
heavenwards, where a Greater Love, which forgives everything and
never feels abandoned, was welcoming me back.

BY THE RIVER PIEDRA I SAT DOWN AND WEPT

7 | Sunday

8 | Monday

9 | Tuesday

10 | Wednesday

11 | Thursday

A warrior on the battlefield is fulfilling his destiny,
and he must surrender himself to that.

MANUSCRIPT FOUND IN ACCRA

12 Friday

13 Saturday

The Lord had been generous and had led him to the very brink of
the inevitable, in order to show him that a man needs to choose
—not accept—his destiny.

THE FIFTH MOUNTAIN

14 | Sunday

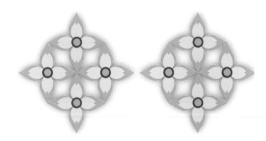

15 Monday

16 Tuesday

17 Wednesday

18 Thursday

The truth is what gives us freedom.

CHRONICLE: NOTES WRITTEN IN AIRPORTS

19 Friday

20 Saturday

There are moments when one should act and moments
when one should accept. The warrior knows how to distinguish
between these moments.

MANUAL OF THE WARRIOR OF LIGHT

21 Sunday

22 | Monday

23 | Tuesday

2 4 Wednesday

2 5 Thursday

Always take the decisions you need to take,
even if you're not sure you're doing the right thing.

BRIDA

26 Friday

27 Saturday

We love because Love sets us free, and we say things that we once
never even had the courage to whisper to ourselves.

MANUSCRIPT FOUND IN ACCRA

28 Sunday

29 Monday

30 Tuesday

31 Wednesday

The warrior of light has the sword in his hands.
He is the one who decides what he will do and what he will never
do.

MANUAL OF THE WARRIOR OF LIGHT

SEPTEMBER

Tolerance

Our soul is governed by four invisible forces:
love, death, power and time.
We must love because we are loved by God.
We must be aware of the Unwanted Visitor
if we are fully to understand life.
We must struggle in order to grow, but without becoming
trapped by whatever power we might gain from that,
because we know that such power is worthless.
Finally, we must accept that our soul, although eternal,
is, at this moment, caught in the web of time,
with all its possibilities and limitations.

MANUSCRIPT FOUND IN ACCRA

1 Thursday

Not everyone needs to feel happy all the time.
Besides, no one can be happy all the time.
I need to learn to deal with the reality of life.

ADULTERY

2 Friday

3 Saturday

Love is above everything else,
and there is no hatred in love,
only the occasional mistake.

BRIDA

4 Sunday

5 Monday

6 Tuesday

7 | Wednesday

8 | Thursday

Love is an act of faith in another person, and love's face should always be wrapped in mystery. Love should be experienced and enjoyed all the time, but, if we try to understand it, the magic will vanish.

CHRONICLE: RESPECTING THE MYSTERY

9 Friday

10 Saturday

Controlling your aggression in order not to harm the other
is the Path of Peace.

ALEPH

11 Sunday

12 Monday

13 Tuesday

14 Wednesday

15 Thursday

The warrior of light is not concerned with results.
He examines his heart and asks: "Did I fight the Good Fight?"
If the answer is "yes," he can rest. If the answer is "no,"
he takes up his sword and begins training all over again.

MANUAL OF THE WARRIOR OF LIGHT

16 Friday

17 Saturday

But do not fight in order to prove that you are right,
or to impose your ideas or ideals on someone else. Accept the fight
only as a way of keeping your spirit clean and your will spotless.
When the fight is over, both sides will emerge as winners because
they tested their limitations and their abilities.

MANUSCRIPT FOUND IN ACCRA

18 | Sunday

19 Monday

20 Tuesday

21 Wednesday

22 Thursday

Sometimes we are gripped by an uncontrollable feeling of sadness.
We realize that the day's magic moment has passed and we did
nothing with it. Then life hides away its magic and its art.

BY THE RIVER PIEDRA I SAT DOWN AND WEPT

23 | Friday

24 | Saturday

Why is Love more important than Faith?
Because Faith is merely the road that leads us to the Greater Love.
Why is Love more important than Charity?
Because Charity is only one of the manifestations of Love.

ADULTERY

25 | Sunday

26 Monday

27 Tuesday

28 Wednesday

29 Thursday

A warrior of light is in the world in order to help his fellow man
and not in order to condemn his neighbor.

MANUAL OF THE WARRIOR OF LIGHT

30 | Friday

A warrior always knows what is worth fighting for.
He never gets embroiled in pointless battles,
and never wastes his time on provocations.

THE FIFTH MOUNTAIN

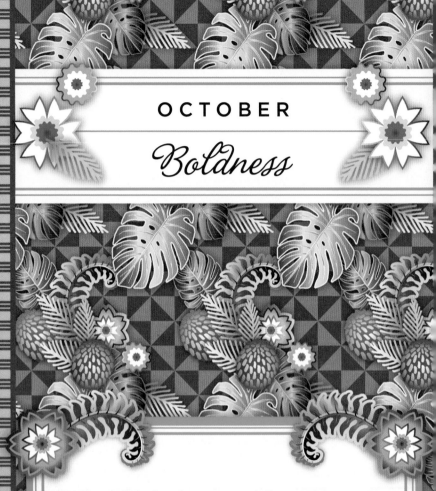

OCTOBER

Boldness

The truth is that the great revolutions and the great advances made by humanity were made by people like us, the only difference being that they had the courage to make a key decision when times were difficult.

CHRONICLE:
IN SEARCH OF THE PERFECT LEADER

1 Saturday

2 | Sunday

Going after a dream has a price. It may mean abandoning our
habits, it may make us go through hardships,
or it may lead us to disappointment, et cetera.
But however costly it may be, it is never as high as the price paid
by people who didn't live.

ADULTERY

3 Monday

4 Tuesday

Love has no rules. We can try to follow the rule book,
to control our heart, to determine how we will behave, but that is all
nonsense. The heart decides, and it is what the heart decides
that matters.

BY THE RIVER PIEDRA I SAT DOWN AND WEPT

5 Wednesday

6 Thursday

7 Friday

8 Saturday

9 Sunday

The first great virtue of a person seeking the spiritual path
is courage.

THE VALKYRIES

10 | Monday

11 | Tuesday

Try the impossible. Don't start low down because that's where you are now. Climb those rungs quickly before they take the ladder away. If you're afraid, say a prayer, but carry on.

THE WINNER STANDS ALONE

12 Wednesday

13 Thursday

14 | Friday

15 | Saturday

16 | Sunday

Making war is not a sin. Making war is an act of love.
The Enemy develops and improves us.

THE PILGRIMAGE

17 Monday

18 Tuesday

Rather than speaking to him of the solace of security,
it teaches him the joy of facing new challenges.

MANUSCRIPT FOUND IN ACCRA

19 Wednesday

20 Thursday

21 Friday

22 Saturday

2 3 Sunday

The moment we decide to face up to a problem,
we realize that we are far more capable than we thought.

THE ZAHIR

24 Monday

25 Tuesday

Be like the fountain that overflows,
not like the cistern that merely contains.

VERONIKA DECIDES TO DIE

26 Wednesday

27 Thursday

28 Friday

29 Saturday

30 Sunday

31 Monday

What kills the relationship between two people is precisely the lack
of challenges, the feeling that nothing is new anymore.
We must continue to be a surprise for each other.

ADULTERY

NOVEMBER

Patience

Walk neither faster nor slower than your own soul,
because it is your soul that will teach you the usefulness of
each step you take. Sometimes taking part in a great battle
will be the thing that will help to change the course of
history. But sometimes you can do that simply by smiling,
for no reason, at someone you happen to pass on the street.

MANUSCRIPT FOUND IN ACCRA

1 Tuesday

2 Wednesday

3 Thursday

Life offers us thousands of opportunities for learning.
Every man and every woman, in every day of our lives,
always has a good opportunity to surrender to Love.
Life is not a long vacation, but a constant learning process.

ADULTERY

4 Friday

5 Saturday

This gift belongs to whoever wishes to accept it.
You have only to believe, accept and not be afraid
of making a few mistakes.

BY THE RIVER PIEDRA I SAT DOWN AND WEPT

6 Sunday

7 | Monday

8 | Tuesday

9 Wednesday

10 Thursday

Can a man remove from his heart the pain of loss?
No, but he can take joy in something won.

THE FIFTH MOUNTAIN

11 Friday

12 Saturday

Let us first seek Love, and everything else will be added.

ADULTERY

13 Sunday

14 Monday

15 Tuesday

16 | Wednesday

17 | Thursday

A warrior of light does not waste his time listening to provocations;
he has a destiny to fulfill.

MANUAL OF THE WARRIOR OF LIGHT

18 Friday

19 Saturday

In order not to suffer, you have to renounce love.

BRIDA

20 | Sunday

21 Monday

22 Tuesday

23 Wednesday

24 Thursday

Love cannot be desired because it is an end in itself.
It cannot betray because it has nothing to do with possession.
It cannot be held prisoner because it is like a river
and will overflow its banks.

THE WITCH OF PORTOBELLO

25 Friday

26 Saturday

God has always offered me another opportunity in life.
You are that opportunity and will help me find my path again.

BY THE RIVER PIEDRA I SAT DOWN AND WEPT

27 | Sunday

28 Monday

29 Tuesday

30 | Wednesday

Respect the time between sowing and harvesting.
Then await the miracle of the transformation.

MANUSCRIPT FOUND IN ACCRA

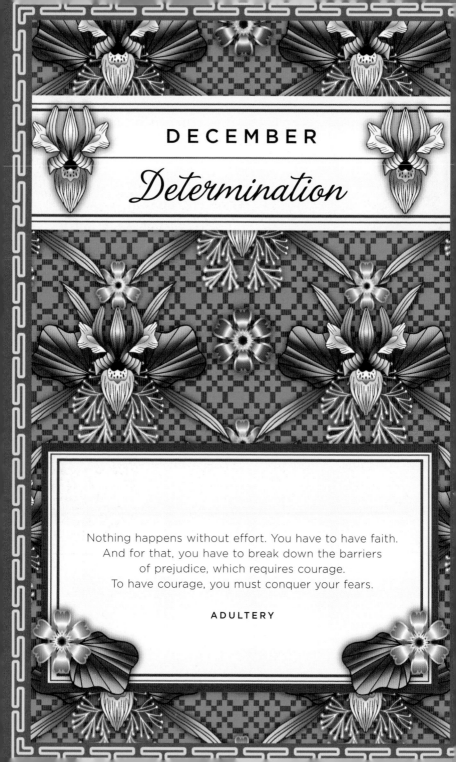

DECEMBER

Determination

Nothing happens without effort. You have to have faith.
And for that, you have to break down the barriers
of prejudice, which requires courage.
To have courage, you must conquer your fears.

ADULTERY

1 Thursday

Our great goal in life is to love.
The rest is silence.

MANUSCRIPT FOUND IN ACCRA

2 | Friday

3 | Saturday

A divided kingdom cannot withstand the attacks of the Enemy.
A divided human being cannot face life with dignity.

BY THE RIVER PIEDRA I SAT DOWN AND WEPT

4 Sunday

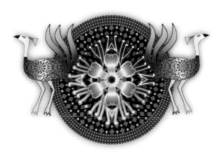

5 Monday

6 Tuesday

7 | Wednesday

8 | Thursday

Imagine a warrior, in the middle of a battle,
pausing to decide which would be the best blow to deliver.
He would die instantly.

THE ZAHIR

9 Friday

10 Saturday

Instead of cursing the place where you fell, first,
find what it was that made you fall.

CHRONICLE: STORIES FROM LATIN AMERICA

11 Sunday

12 Monday

13 Tuesday

14 Wednesday

15 Thursday

There are many ways to serve the Lord.
If you feel that this is your destiny, then go in search of it.
Only someone who is happy can spread happiness.

BY THE RIVER PIEDRA I SAT DOWN AND WEPT

16 Friday

17 Saturday

She knew the path to follow, and she must follow it to the end.
She knew that if she gave up now, she would find it harder
and harder to make any choices in life.

BRIDA

18 | Sunday

19 | Monday

20 | Tuesday

21 | Wednesday

22 | Thursday

Whoever you are or whatever you do,
when you really want something,
it's because that desire was born in the soul of the Universe.
That is your mission on Earth.

THE ALCHEMIST

2 3 | Friday

2 4 | Saturday

The gates of Paradise stand open for those determined to enter.
The world is in the hands of those who have the courage to dream
and to live out their dreams.

THE VALKYRIES

25 Sunday

26 Monday

27 Tuesday

28 Wednesday

29 Thursday

If the warrior of light thinks only of his goal,
he will not be able to pay attention to the signs along the way.

MANUAL OF THE WARRIOR OF LIGHT

30 Friday

31 Saturday

I am a mystery to myself; I opened the floodgates
and I want to go further, try everything that I know exists...

ADULTERY

Original title: *Coragem 2016*

Copyright © 2015 Paulo Coelho and Forlagshuset Bazar AS
http://paulocoelhoblog.com/

Published by arrangement with Sant Jordi Asociados, Agencia Literaria, S.L.U., Barcelona (Spain). www.santjordi-asociados.com

All rights reserved. Published in the United States of America by Vintage Books, a division of Penguin Random House LLC, New York, and in Canada by Random House of Canada Ltd., Toronto, Penguin Random House Companies.

Vintage is a registered trademark and Vintage International and Colophon are trademarks of Penguin Random House LLC.

Vintage ISBN: 978-1-101-91231-7

Quote selection: Márcia Botelho
Translation copyright © Margaret Jull Costa
Illustrations by Catalina Estrada, www.catalinaestrada.com
Author photograph © Paul Macleod
Design by Lene Stangebye Geving / Mercè Roig

www.vintagebooks.com

Printed and bound by TBB, Eslovaquia, 2015

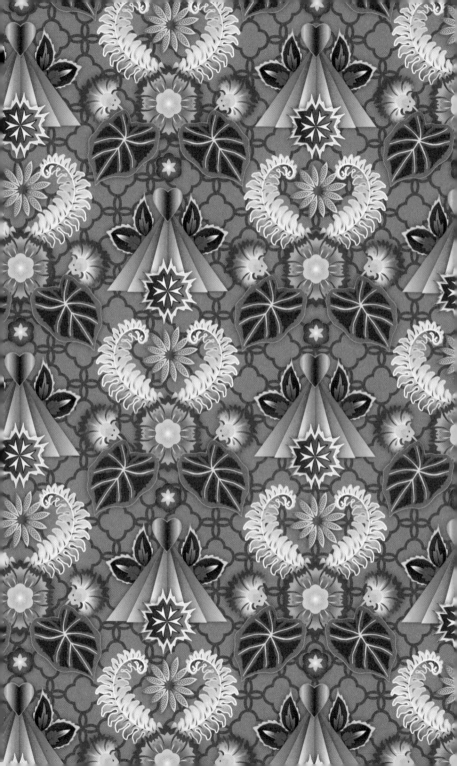